Charles Burney

Preludes, fugues, and interludes, for the organ:

Alphabetically arranged in all the keys that are most perfectly in tune

upon that instrument, & printed in a pocket size for the convenience of

young organists, for whose use this book is particularly

Charles Burney

Preludes, fugues, and interludes, for the organ:
Alphabetically arranged in all the keys that are most perfectly in tune upon that instrument, & printed in a pocket size for the convenience of young organists, for whose use this book is particularly

ISBN/EAN: 9783337807849

Printed in Europe, USA, Canada, Australia, Japan

Cover: Foto ©ninafisch / pixelio.de

More available books at **www.hansebooks.com**

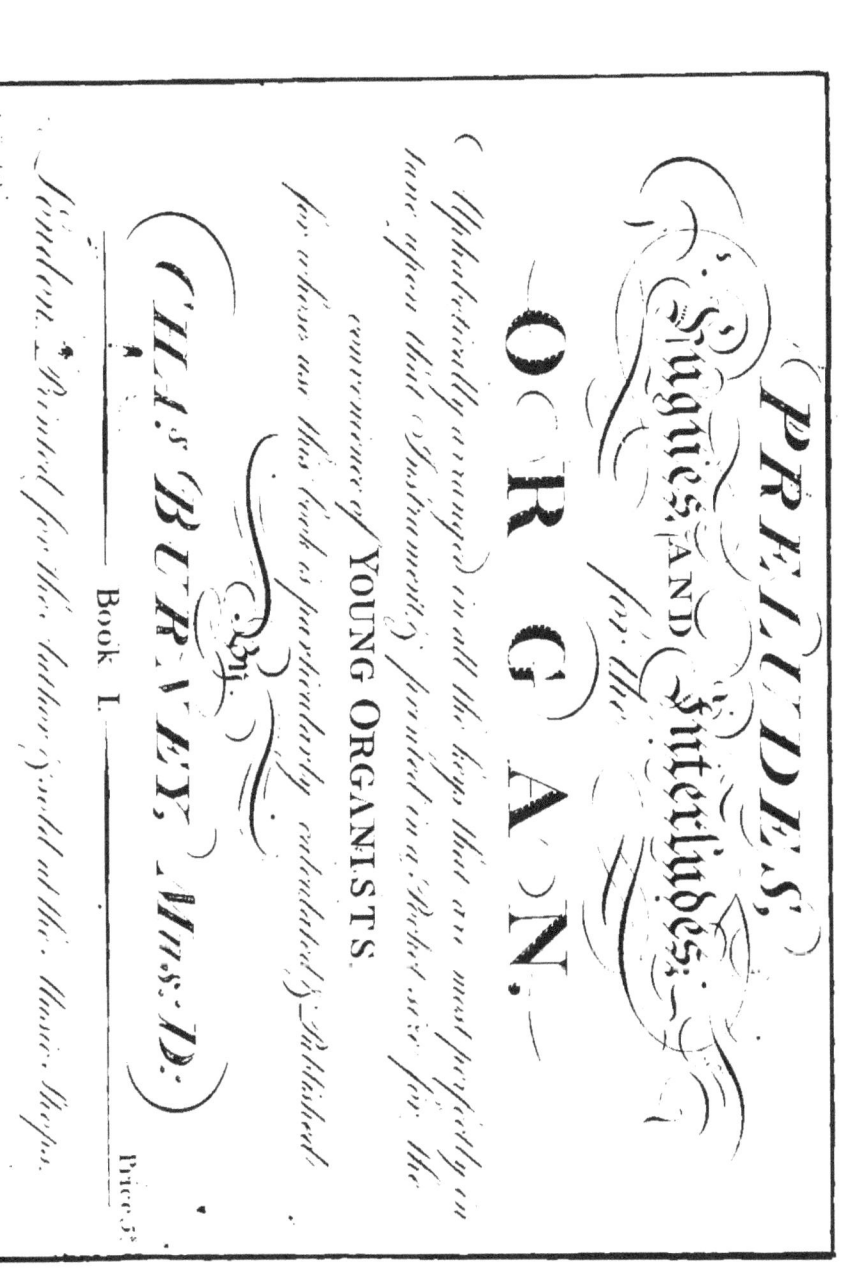

PRELUDES,
Fugues, AND Interludes;
for the
ORGAN.

Alphabetically arranged in all the keys that are most perfectly in tune upon that Instrument; pointed in a Pocket size for the convenience of YOUNG ORGANISTS.

for whose use this book is particularly calculated & Published

By

CHAS BURNEY Mus: D:

Book I.

Price 5s.

London. Printed for the Author, & sold at the Music Shops.

Introduction

Andante

1

Fuga

Allegro

A

4 Interlude, Fughetta.

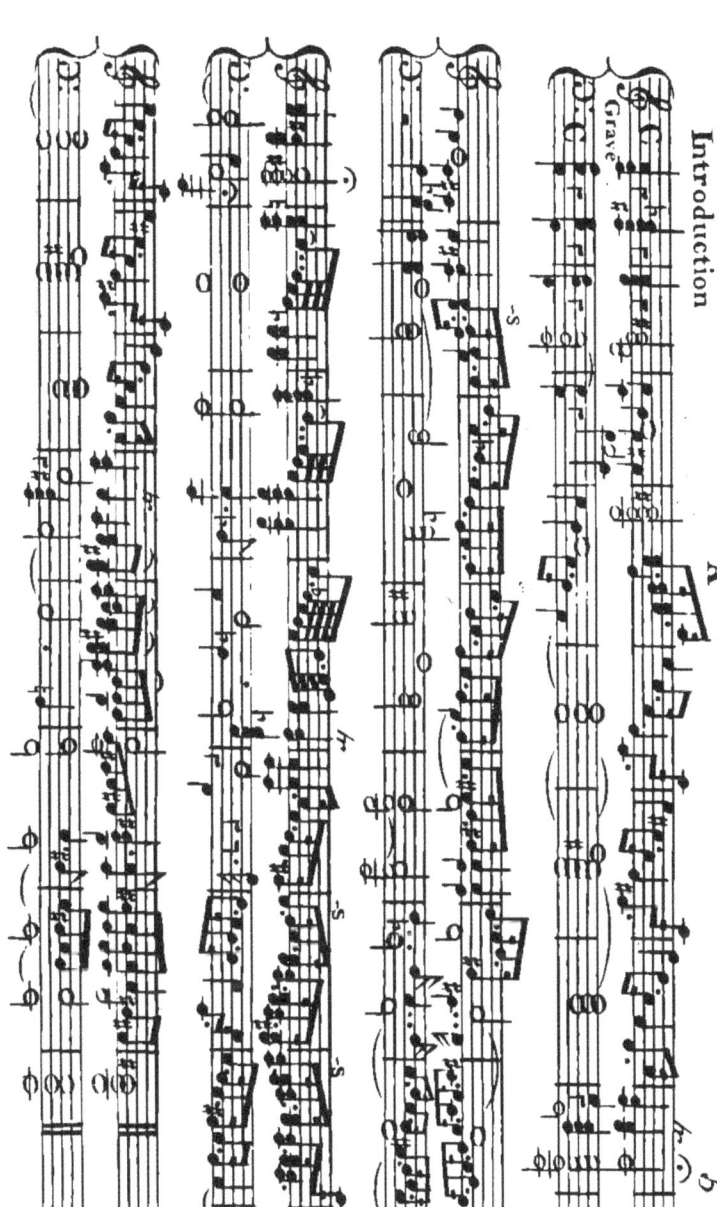

Fuga Allegro

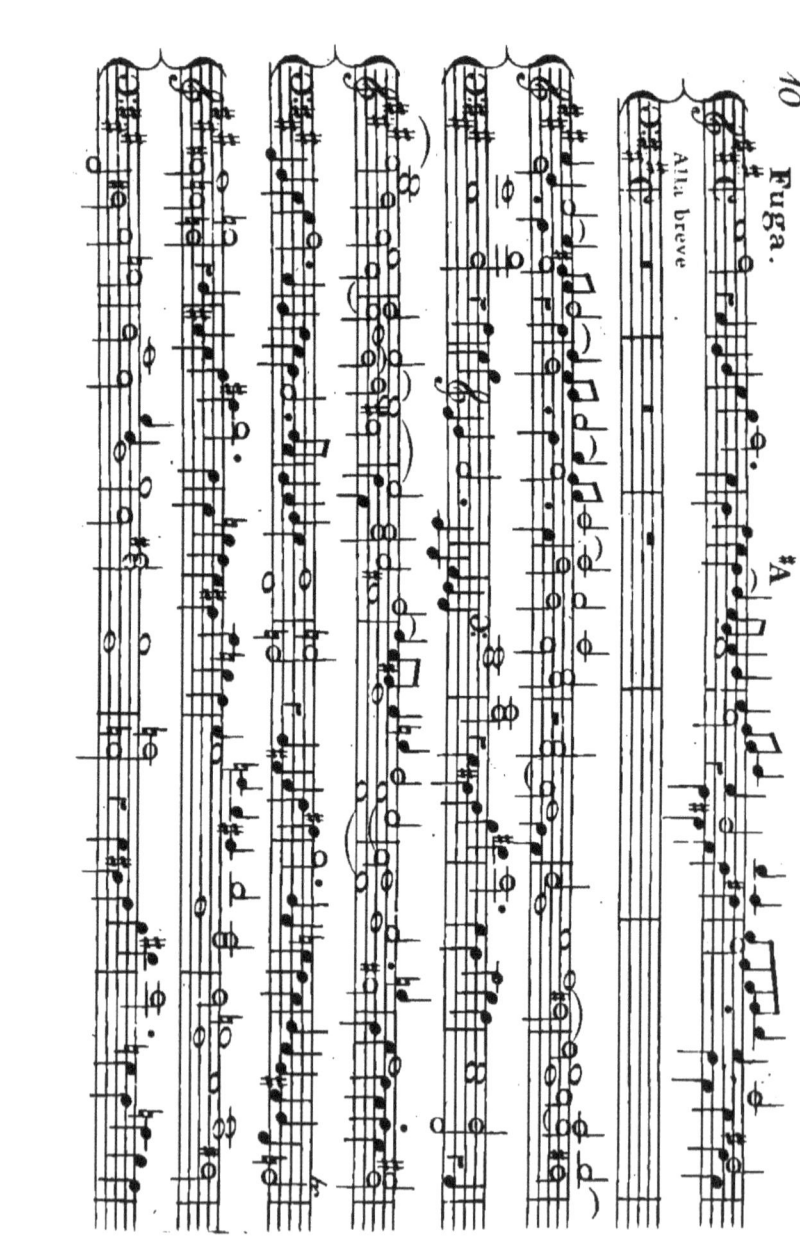

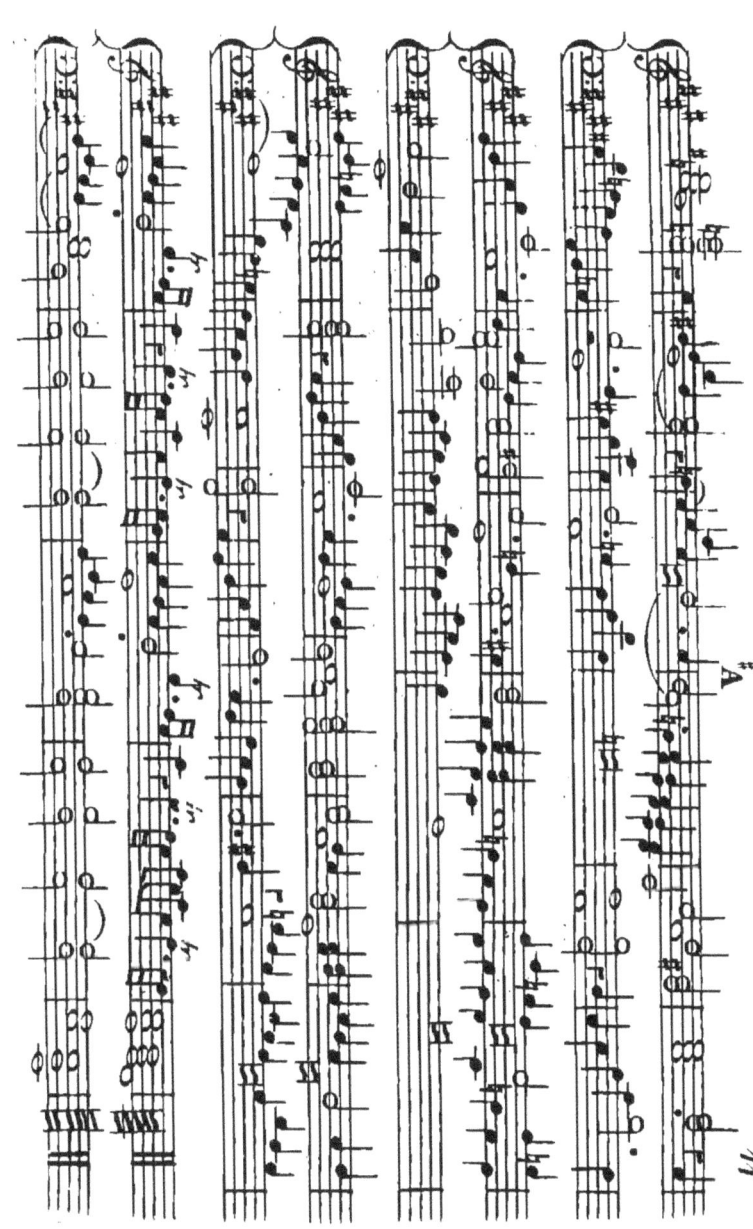

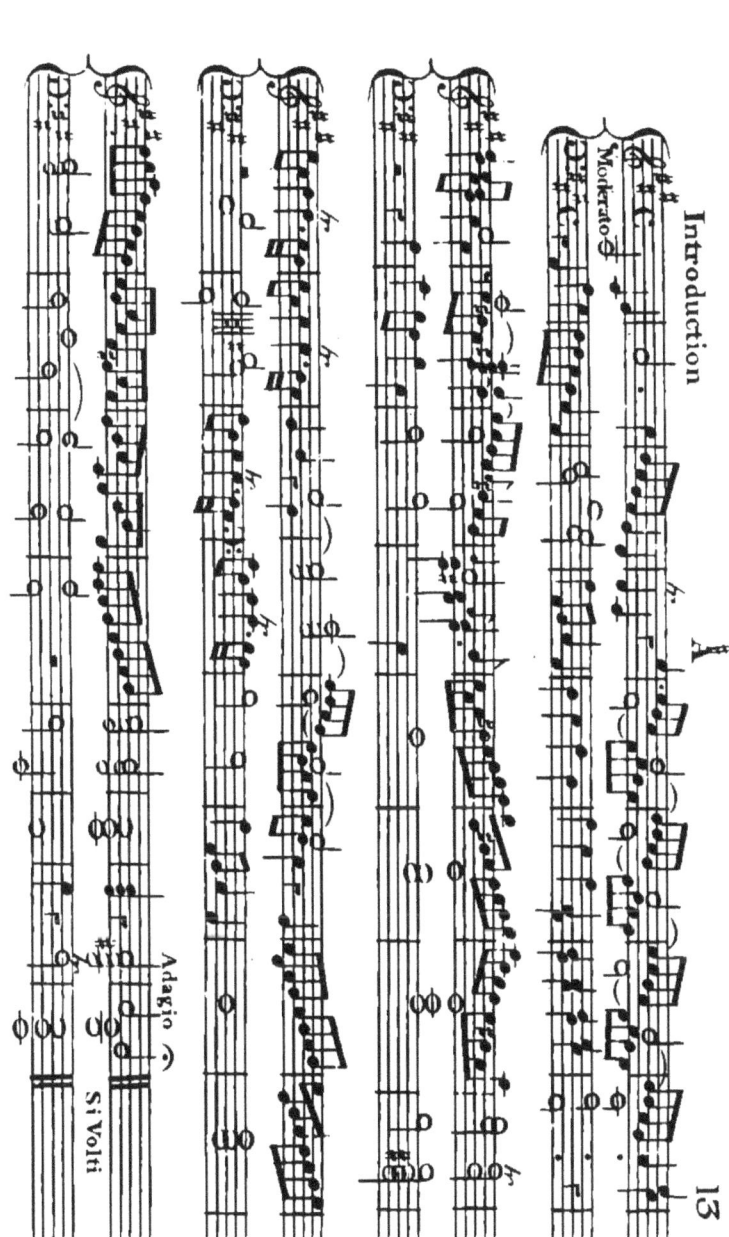

Fuga.

Allegro.

A

Adagio

A #

15

16   Introduction   B♭

Andante

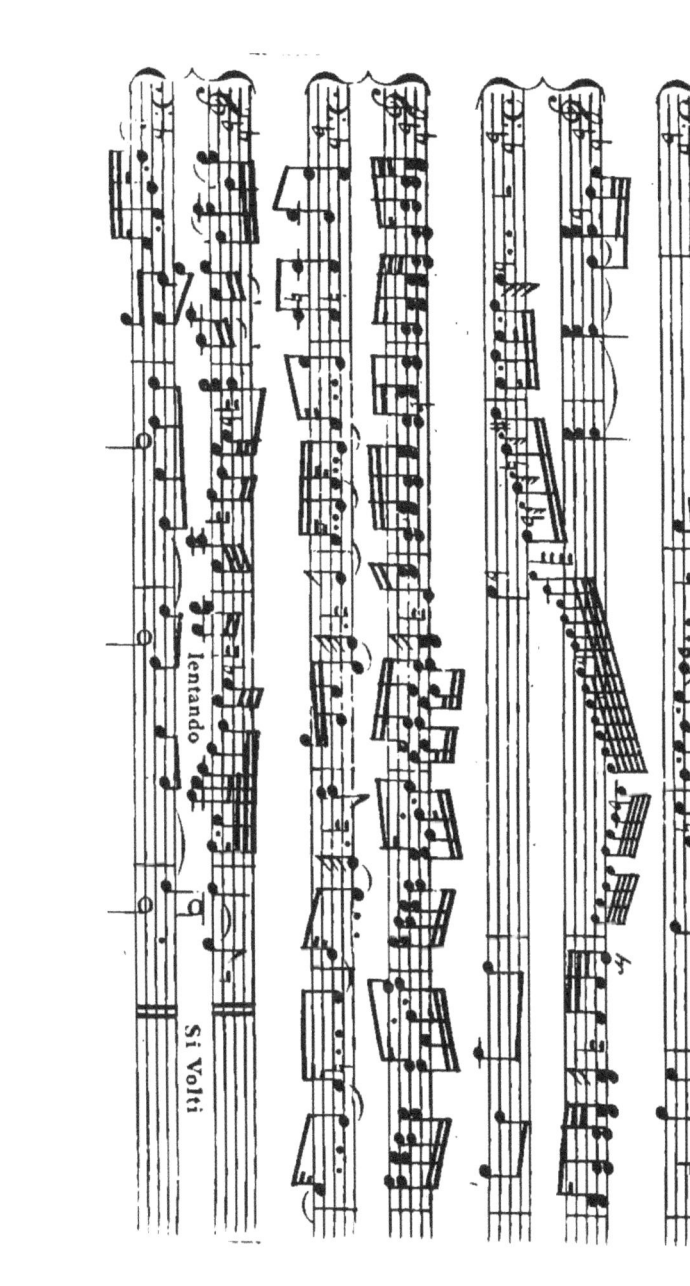

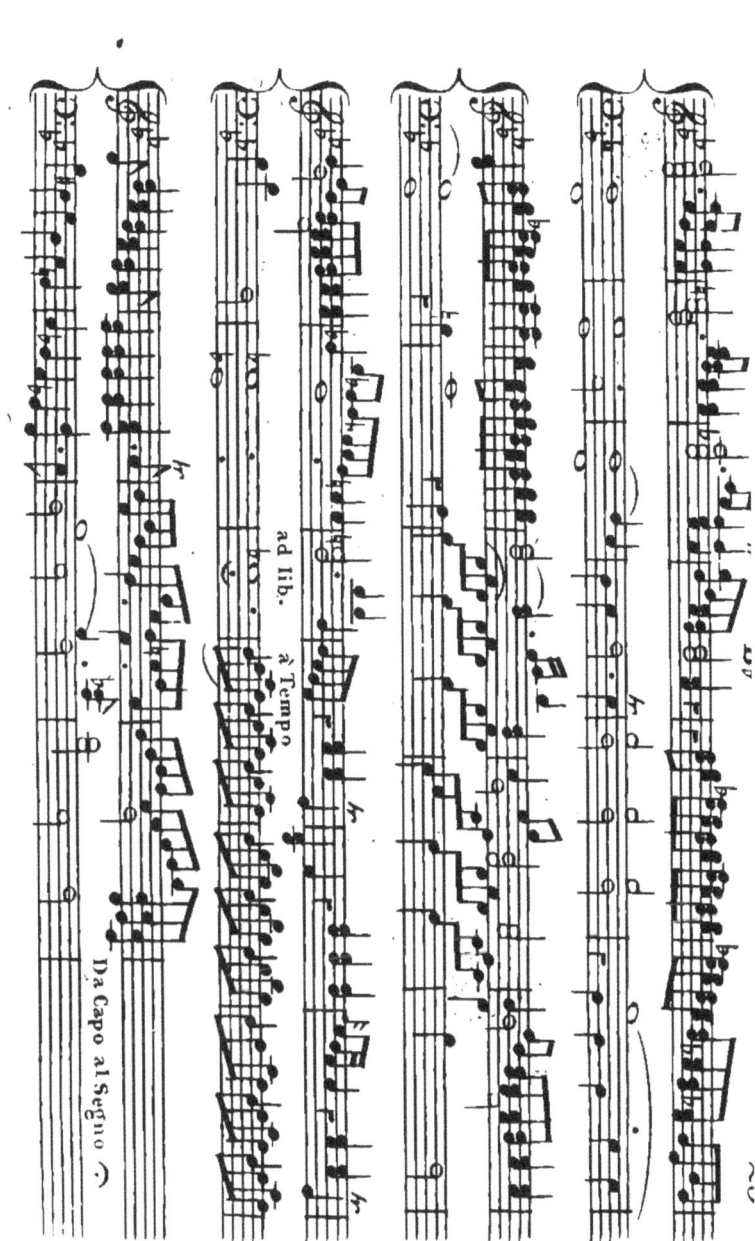

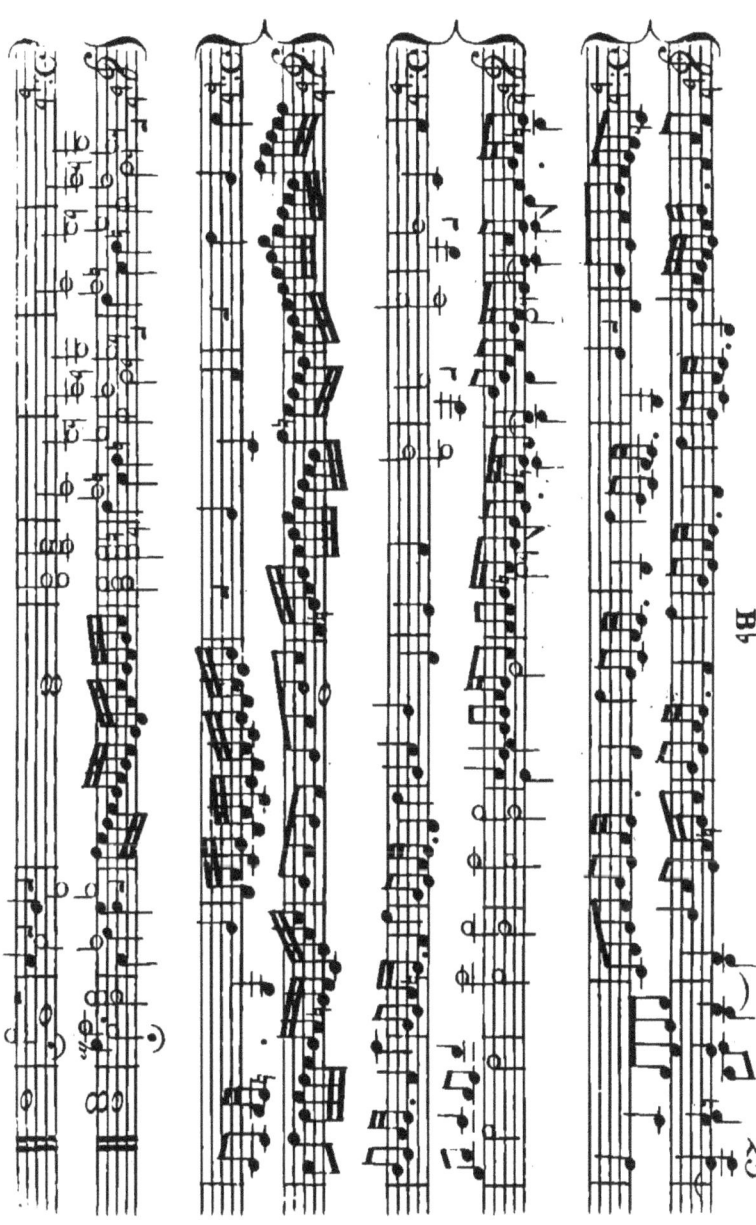

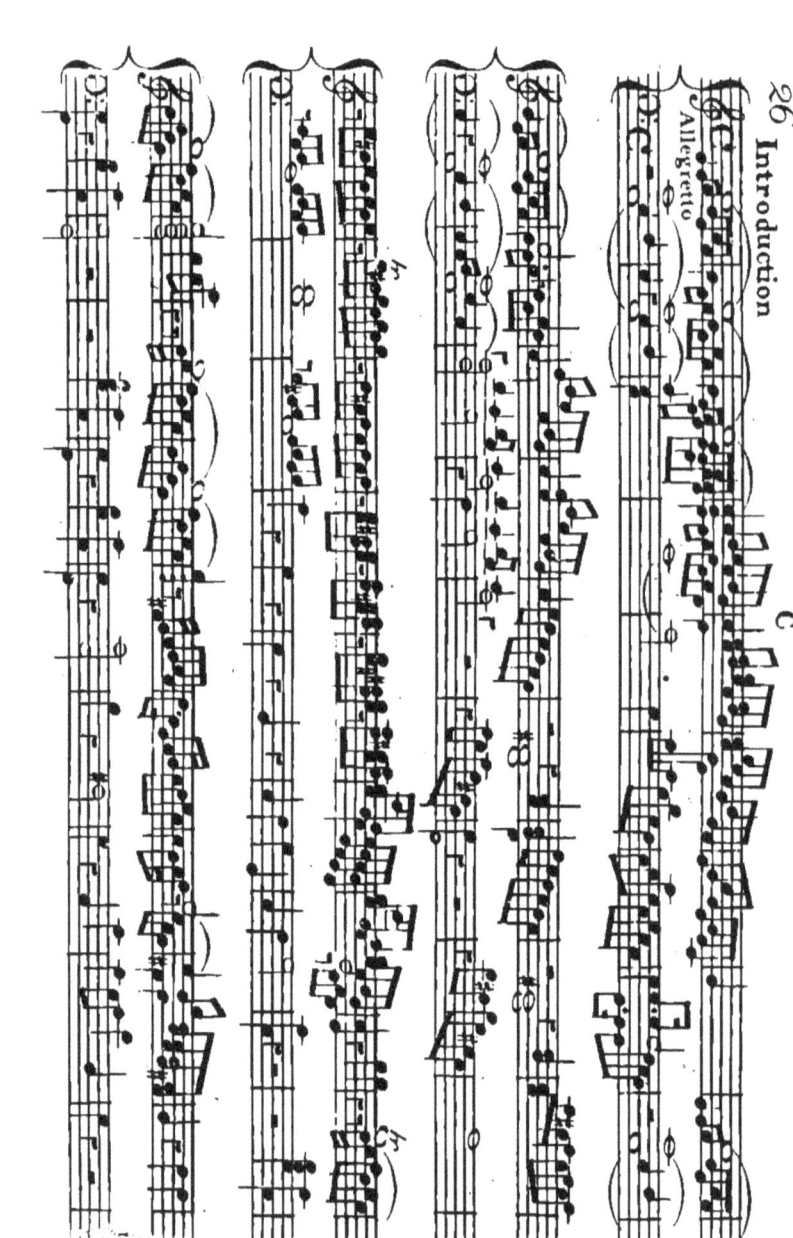

Allegretto

Introduction

Adagio

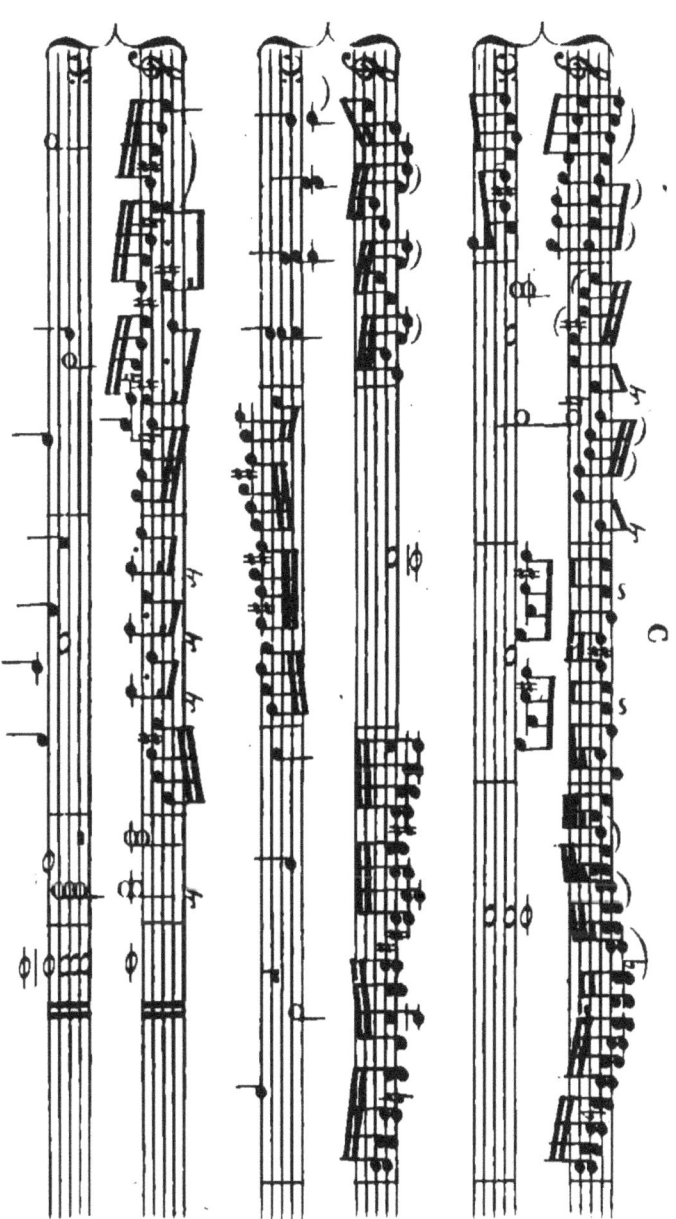

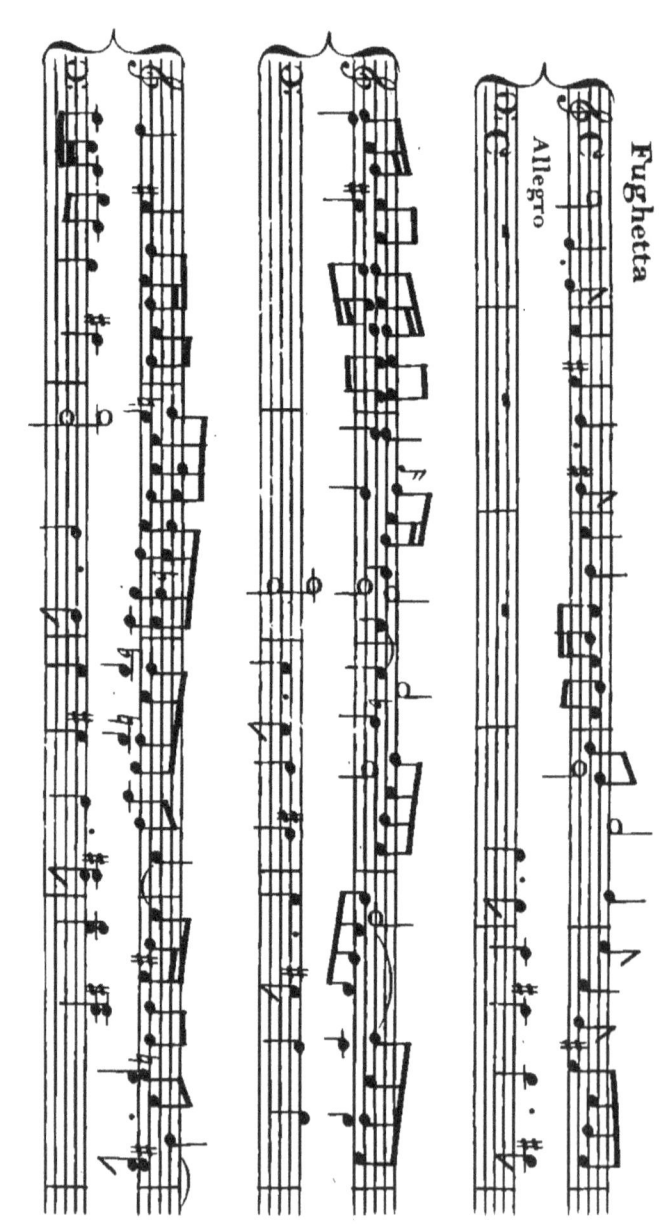

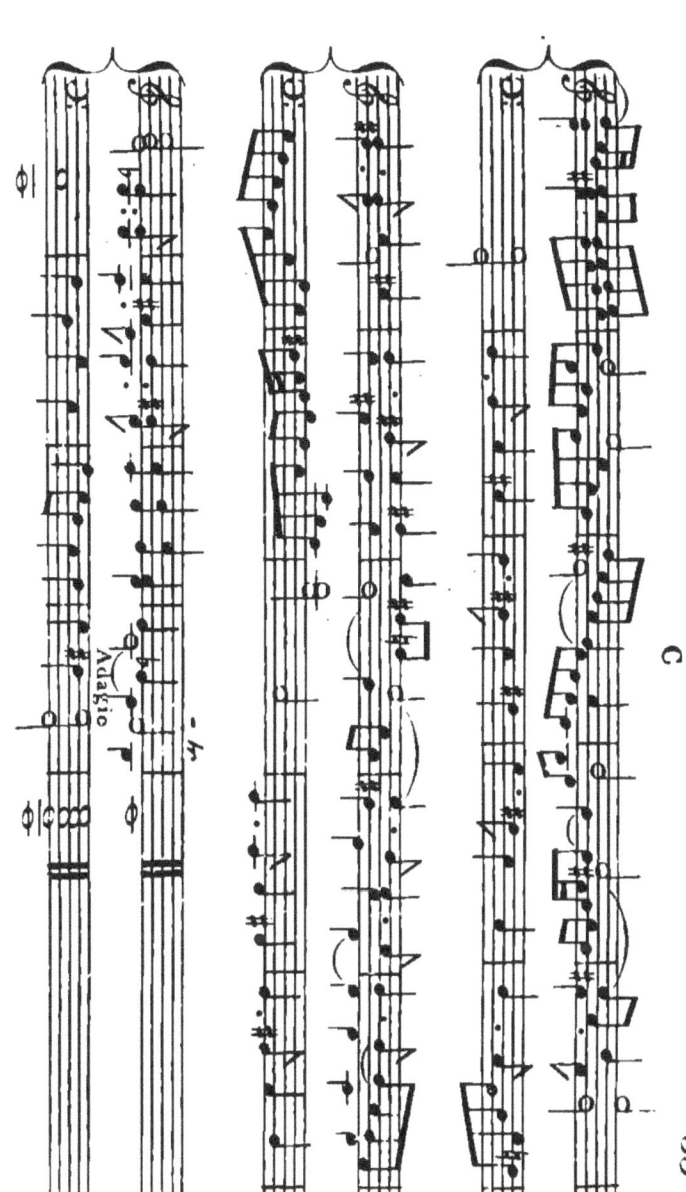

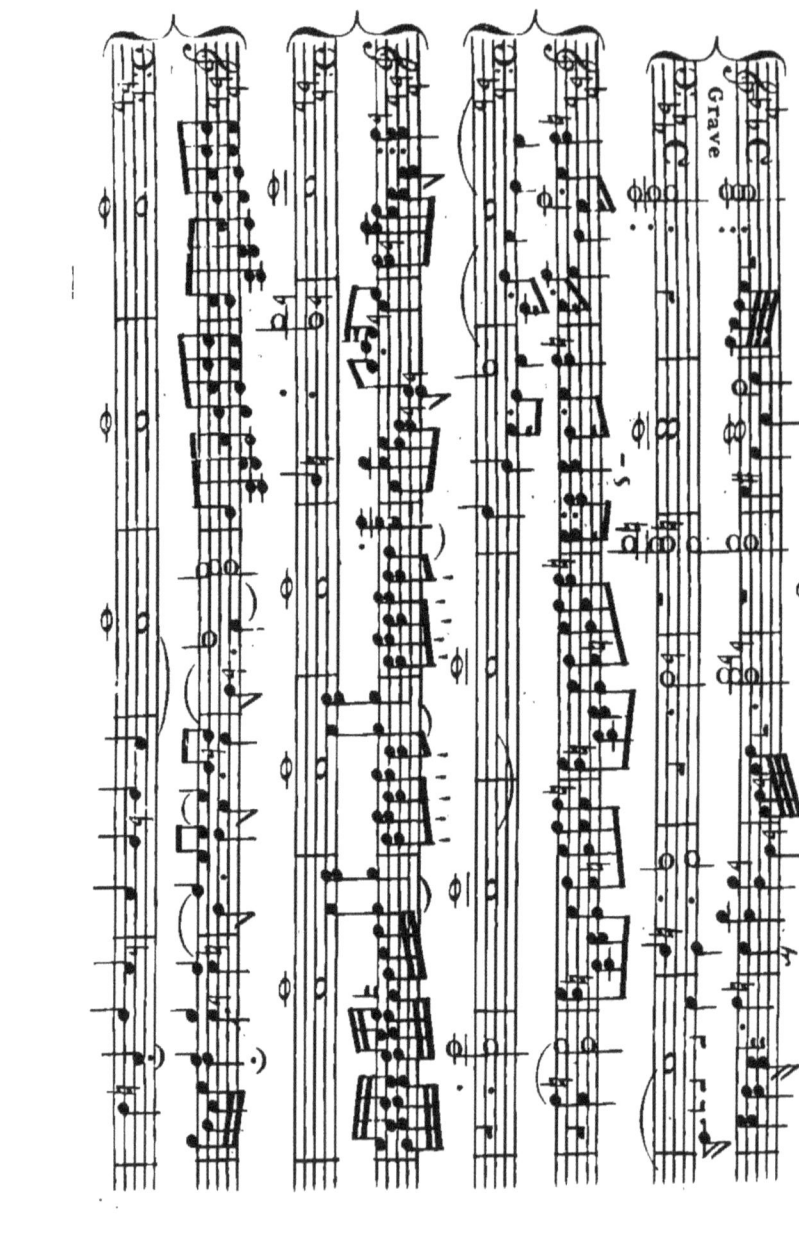

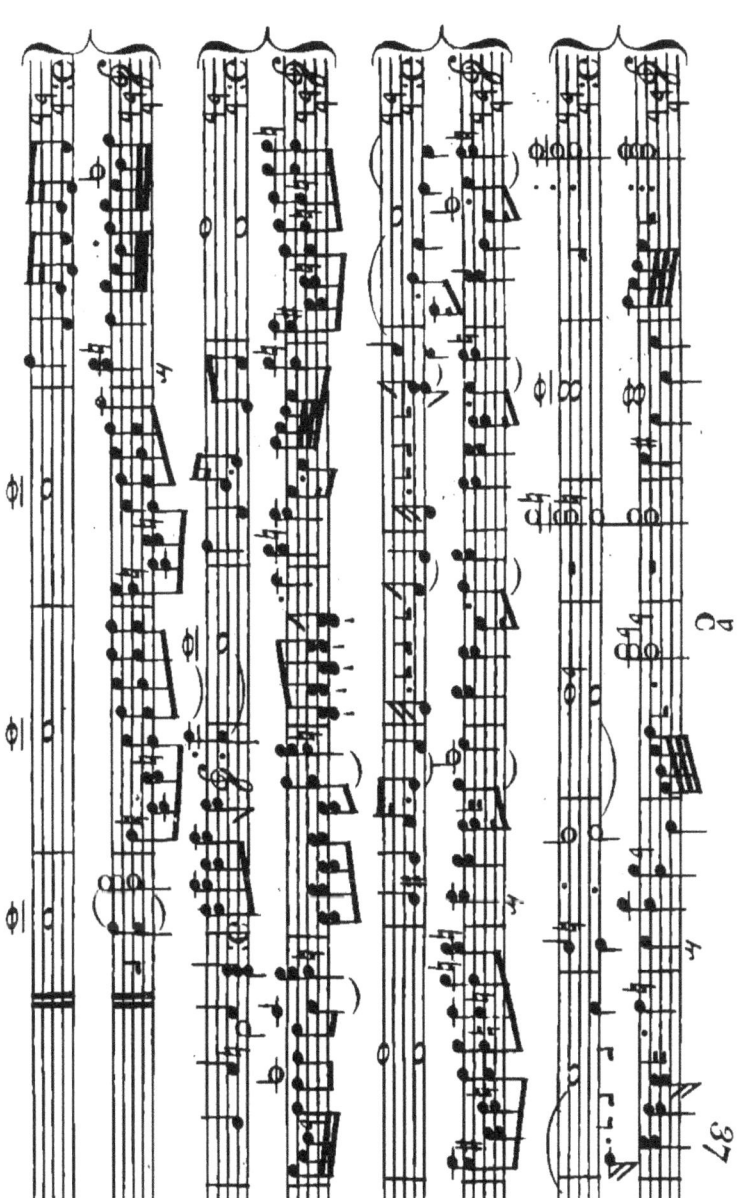

37

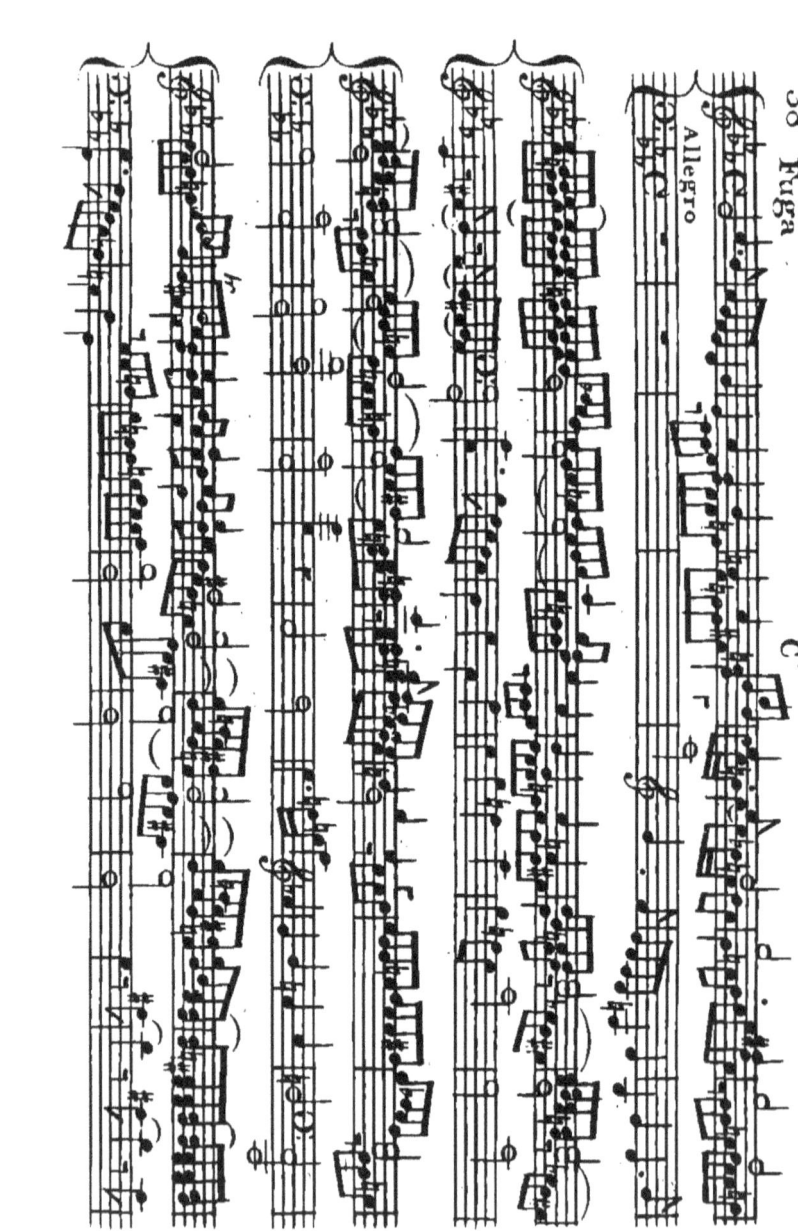

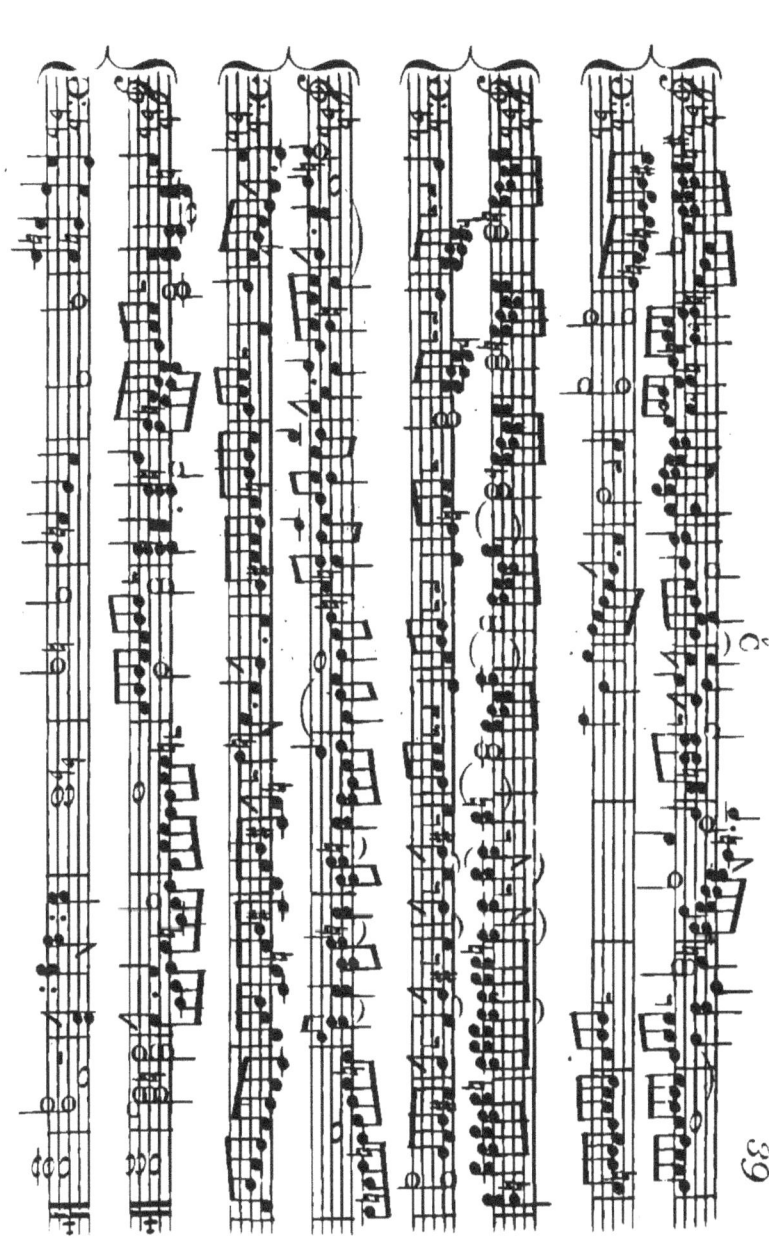

39

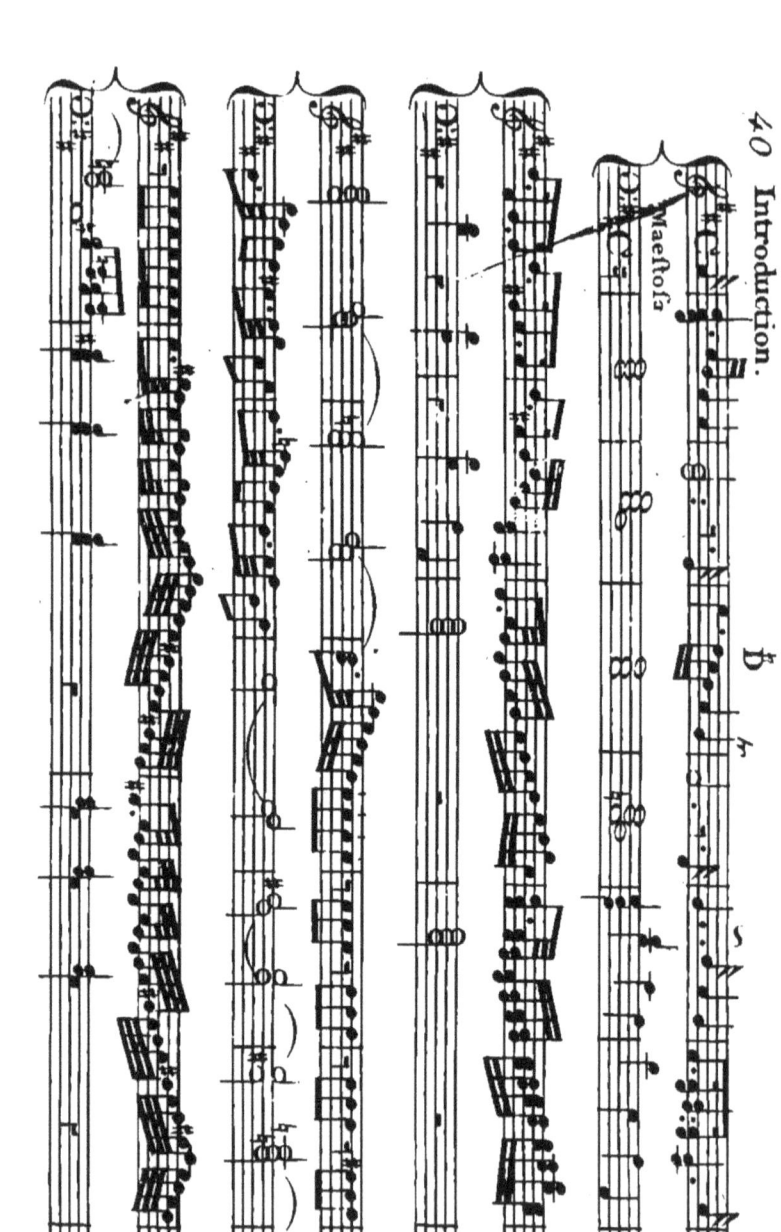

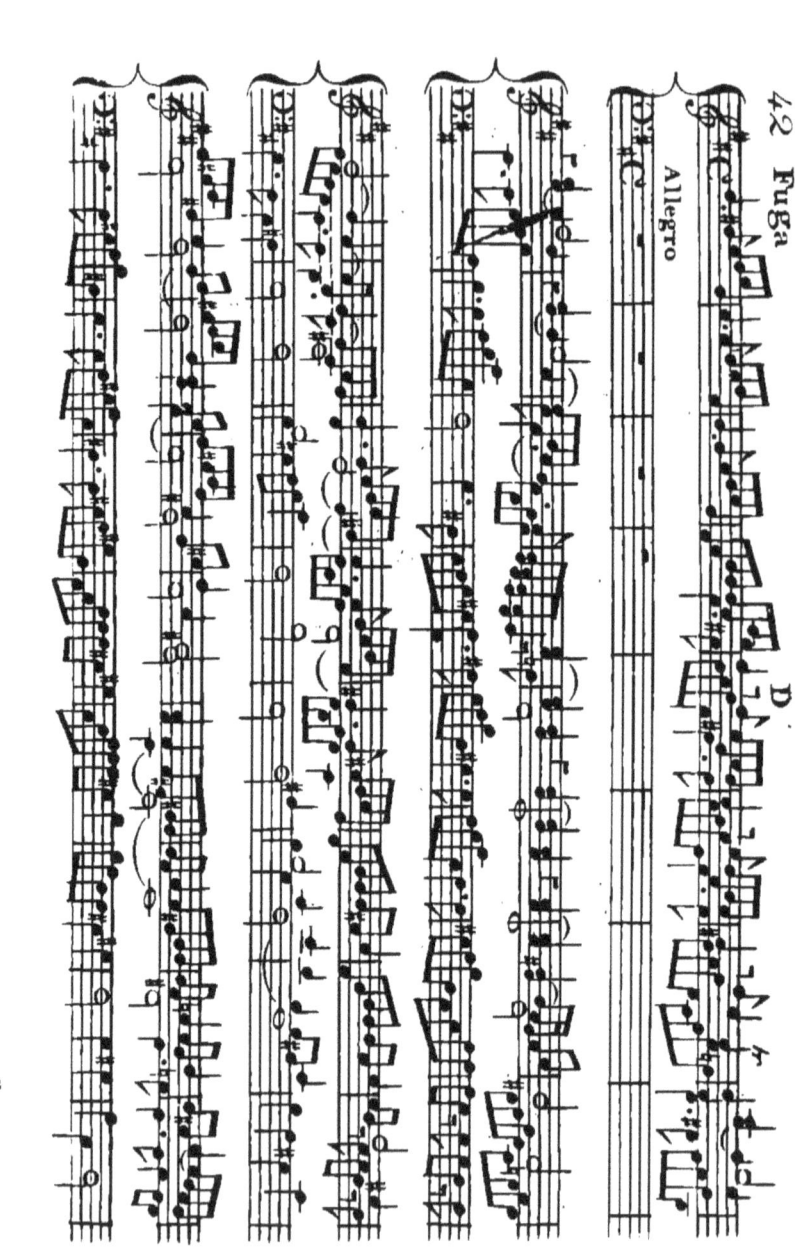

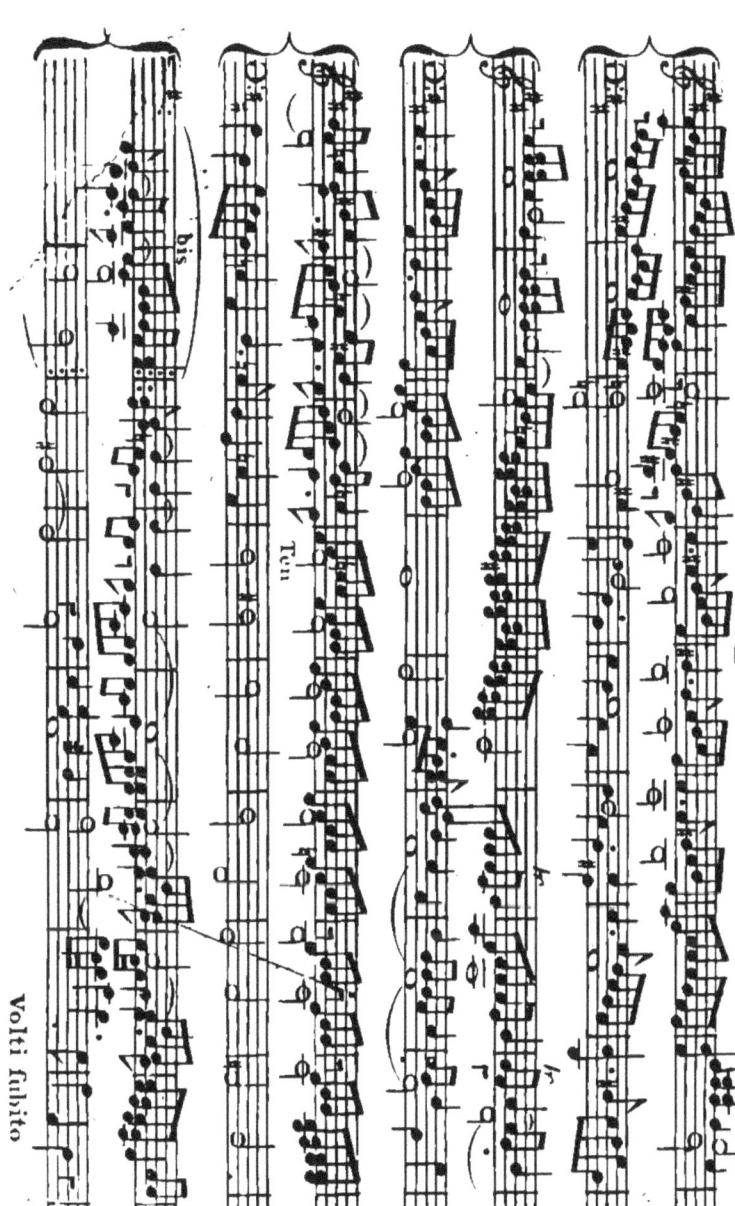

FINIS

www.ingramcontent.com/pod-product-compliance
Lightning Source LLC
Chambersburg PA
CBHW021434090426
42739CB00009B/1476